Classic Chapbooks
Bart Solarczyk

Other books from Redhawk Publications:

All I Wanted by Jake Young

Birdhouse by Clayton Joe Young and Tim Peeler

The Bost-Burrus House by G. Leroy Lail and Richard Eller

Bouquets Hadn't Been Invented Yet by Tony Deal

Food Culture Recipes from the Henry River Mill Village

From Darkness: The Fated Soules Series, Book One by Jan Lindie

Going To Wings by Sandra Worsham

The Hickory Furniture Mart: A Landmark History by G. Leroy Lail and Richard Eller

Hickory: Then & Now by Richard Eller and Tammy Panther

Hickory: Then & Now The Complete Texts by Richard Eller

Hickory: Then & Now The Complete Photograph Collection

Hurdles by Ric Vandett

The Legends of Harper House – The Shuler Era by Richard Eller

More by Shelby Stephenson

Mother Lover Child & Me by Erin Anthony

Newton: Then & Now by Richard Eller and Sylvia Kidd Ray

Piedmont The Jazz Rat Of Cunningham Park by Mike Bruner

A Place Where Trees had Names by Les Brown

Polio, Pitchforks & Perseverance by Richard Eller

Sanctuary Art Journal 2018, 2019, 2020

Secrets I'm Dying to Tell You by Terry Barr

Sittin' In with the Sun by Carter Monroe

Sky Full of Stars and Dreams by Scott Owens

Sleeping Through the Graveyard Shift by Al Maginnes

Suffragettes by Harriett Bannon and Brigette Hadley

Waffle House Blues by Carter Monroe

We Might As Well Eat by Terry Barr

We See What We Want to See: The Henry River Mill Village in Poetry, Photography, and History by Clayton Joe Young and Tim Peeler

What Came to Me—Collected Columns Vol One by Arlene Neal

Win/Win by G. Leroy Lail

Classic Chapbooks

Walt Whitman's Watching

Haiku from Old Fedora

Blues

Right Direction

Bart Solarczyk

REDHAWK
PUBLICATIONS

Copyright © 2021 by Bart Solarczyk

Published by REDHAWK PUBLICATIONS
2550 US Hwy 70 SE
Hickory NC 28602

Robert Canipe, Publisher and Senior Editor
Tim Peeler, Editor
Patty Thompson, Project and Permissions Coordinator

All rights reserved. This book or parts thereof may not be reproduced in any form, stored in any retrieval system, or transmitted in any form by any means—electronic, mechanical, photocopy, recording, or otherwise—without prior written permission of the publisher, except as provided by United States of America copyright law. For permission requests, write to the publisher, at "Attention: Permissions Coordinator," at the address above.

ISBN: 978-1-952485-25-1

Part One
Walt Whitman's Watching

Originally published by Pudding House Publications, 2005

In Memory of Cait Collins

The Prodigal Word
(for Glenn)

The poem
walks with you
then suddenly
it's gone

don't search
sit tight
it can never
live alone

when it
wanders home
drink hard & kill
the fatted calf

eat fast
its fickle heart
beats only
to break you

Sweet Thing

We share this small
sweet thing
before we're captured
by the day's hard drone

meet me here again
when the sun drops low

we'll test each tear
against the moon's
silver promise.

Wings

My doctor dreams
he's a bird

drops feathers
on my blanket

puffed & tickled
in the sun

my medicine hat
my cracked egg skull.

The Job

You come here I'm crazy
pet my baby crocodile
wax my sinful back
& shave my demons

cured pink & bald
let's do this more often
tomorrow's not good
how about yesterday?

Cosmic Hangover

Shit rises

to our ears

& you sit there

eating soup

if we hadn't

killed God

you'd never

be forgiven.

Catholic School

I painted rocks
with salamander blood

God died
above my desk

crows hopped
on hardwood floors

in sexless
shoes.

Wonderland

Shattering
the looking glass

bleeding into sleep
& still no Alice.

Sister in Black

(for Cait)

Sister in black
pierced tongue temptress
queen of the underground

come mother
my sweet sorrow
& hold me once again

I've been drinking
I've been scribbling
I've been trying on new socks

open wide
& let those crazy words
slide home.

Redemption Song

The man who pissed spiders
now walks among us healed

he rejoices as the wicked
fist their stones.

Walt Whitman's Watching

We sweat & we wipe
work the world's rhythm
sway with the grass & leaves

we drink the day's end
ignore the astronomer
gazing the stars in our cups

we speak what we will
across cyberspace
bold water, flesh & air

so snuggle up
take off your clothes
let me write a poem on you.

Wood
(for David)

The carpenter
knows wood

from the manger
to the cross

the table
& the thorn

the gavel
& the common cup

nailed fast
to every last chance

the carpenter
knows wood.

Poem Angel

Poem angel flying drunk
won't you please call home?

you were gone
before I wrote you down.

Days Like These
(for Ron)

We are all
wounded healers

bad dreams
interwoven

dead
fish

with dead
fish eyes.

Television

Born without sin
on a beautiful planet

& this is how
we choose to live.

She Has No Nose

Dear Miss Lonely Heart
I've fallen off the page

my feet keep swelling up
& I'm dumb as Baby Jesus

so many sad people
to feel sorry for

a pot of black & white
where the rainbow ends.

The Good Thief
(for Marko)

A man once sang forgiveness
while drinking his own blood

he picked death's lock
& the good thief stole heaven.

October Boy

I light my pipe
blow smoke rings
that stretch into
Halloween faces

be not afraid
my children

see how the
jack-o-lantern
smiles

his empty
head burning.

Dogma

God chained
in the backyard

barking barking barking
with no teeth.

Dear Wife

If I fall

into a coma

& you find me

on the floor

in the morning

zip me up

& make me clean

for the authorities

my secrets

are your secrets

those vows

in sickness

& in health.

Someday

Someday I'll write
an epic poem

long lines
thick pages

my very own
Iliad & Odyssey

but tonight let's agree
to settle for this

you see the job
keeps kicking my ass

& right now
I'm painlessly drunk

& I never said today
would be someday.

Sniper Clowns

Sniper clowns
are in my yard

they climb trees
they're on the roof

sniper clowns
aren't here

to make
me happy.

PART TWO

Haiku from *Old Fedora*

Originally published in Old Fedora *Special Issue Number One, 2003*

I can't name the year
my mother
last cooked me an egg

Banging my balls
with an empty
I grow strong

Burn a thousand

poems

keep this one

Reading my e-mail

I worry

my penis is too small

Changing socks
I remember
Christ walked everywhere

Broken plant
smoking
what she left me

Summer long
barefoot girls
tempt my fetish

The kid
who ate his boogers
sells me insurance

All those

temporary beers

pissed away

Walking Otis hatless

rain

on my bald head

Ten hours worth
of Rolling Rock
fumbling for my pipe

Blue morning
shaving
Monday's face

Sudden rain
butterfly
kisses leaf

Loving the crow
I inch
toward murder

Dirty ashtray beach
beer cap bent like smiling clam
listen—I am God

Bricks dropped like old friends
young & drunk I pissed here
once
thinking of that now

Broken Arrow Ranch
full moon—electric guitars
Shakey lays it down

That bastard bug!
killed it
with bare hands

PART THREE

Blues

Originally published in Peshekee River Special *No. 2, 2001*

Blues

She leaves you low
as low can go

you're dirt

she never was
a flower.

Blues

She thinks
you can do better

you try

she was wrong
again

Blues

She takes you down
to the low end

this town
bleeds like you

this town
knows your name.

Blues

On the job
on the bus

she's static
she's the soundtrack

this movie needs
a better set of wheels.

Blues

She leaves you
with a stranger

laughing as she
slams the door

skinny fingers
tugging at your fly.

Blues

She watches Psycho
as you trim the Xmas ham

the in-laws
crowd the table

later on
she makes you wear a dress.

Blues

The wheels fall off
you bump along

she's waving
from the fast lane

the red lights in the rear view
are for you.

Blues

She's a life support system
for a cunt

you're a dildo
with a wallet

sometimes it works
sometimes it's better than love.

Blues

She loves
her new perfume

you fart
to clear the air

she never gets your jokes
she never will.

Blues

She sends you out
for cigarettes

you take
the long way home

the world is big
it shrinks along the way.

Blues

She drops you
like a habit

she'll
be back

you're
her favorite monkey.

Blues

She breaks down
every October

it's your favorite
time of year

her colors change
you rake away what dies.

PART FOUR

Right Direction
Originally published by Lilliput Review, *2016*

The Same Big Poem
(for Pat McKinnon)

Seize your portion

clocks run fast

flesh fails

but the word proclaims

loud & stubborn

whispered in love

an epitaph

it's all the same big poem.

The Rules

Kill it

eat it

shit it out

set the clock

get up

begin again.

Phoebe's Gone

A box of ash & rattle

warming in the sun

love is love

even when it pees on the rug.

Meant To Be A Nail

The poem was meant
to be a nail

pounded hard
between the eyes

but I got drunk
& lost the hammer

bear with me
this could take a while.

November clouds
smiling dog
bites the wind

where we

planted her

no flower

I Met This Poem

I met this poem
she had good dope
I bought the beer

we started in
I wrote her down
she said I had her all wrong

we hit it harder
nothing worked
someone had to go

a man dies anyway
but the right poem
is a shadow of forever.

up & down the block

my country

lost in a sea of flags

already sad

crows divide

my sorrow

Early Robins

Orange breasted buddhas

test their beaks

against

the frozen earth

July 1, 2009

Thirteen years ago today
the pain left & you floated
above that bloated sack
your beauty had become

charcoal quilt dragging the moon
my father on the front porch
guarding this city where he loved you
lights go off, lights go on.

For Ron, Happy In His Postmodern Cave

Wrap your wings in walls & curtains

spit your poems into cyberspace

I'd rather we were drinking on Baldheaded Hill

two bugs in the breeze, softly swinging.

Right Direction

Hangover heart
head full of dog smiles
November's circular wind

the blessings of
right direction
with perfect uncertainty.

Haiku

Cats can teach the truth:
purring back to never born
Hal enters heaven.

As Pages Turn

September sneaks in
through the screen door
finds me drunk
& whispers she can't stay.

Dogs

Dogs die old & dogs die young
then sit in memory's shadow

until that big gate swings
& finally you're home.

Pack It Tight
(for Ron Androla)

A bird splatters
the passenger window

blue moose snow
an ash grown dangerously long

take out your teeth, lie down
& dream of highways

pack it tight, I'll drive
you write it down.

Broken On The Wing

A bluebird flies one cage
to claim another

I punch out then
feather home to drink

It's a migratory curse
hollowed in the bones

to bend your neck & peck
before you sing.

Guardrail Graffiti

(a found poem)

DICKNOSE
FUCK YOU
I LOVE DRUGS

quick words
   chopped thoughts -
Ron wants the endless chant

Coda

Three ticks
to midnight

the music
of her bones

Bart Solarczyk lives in Pittsburgh PA where he was born & properly raised. He has one cat, one dog & one daughter. Over the past thirty-eight years his poems have been published in print & online in a variety of magazines, journals, broadsides & anthologies. He is the author of nine poetry chapbooks & the full-length collection *Tilted World* from Low Ghost Press.

www.ingramcontent.com/pod-product-compliance
Lightning Source LLC
Chambersburg PA
CBHW031212090426
42736CB00009B/884